I0846308

# INSTANT ART PRINTS

# POP ART FLOWERS
## COLLECTION

A Journey Through Life and Colours

Photography and design

## Sabrina Martorelli

# PROLOGUE

Welcome to a world where art pulsates with vibrant life and the ordinary transforms into extraordinary—The Pop Art Flowers Collection. Within these vivid pages, a kaleidoscope of colours, bold strokes, and iconic imagery dances to the rhythm of modern culture and innovation.

In an era defined by mass media, consumerism, and the rise of popular culture, Pop Art emerged as a revolutionary movement, challenging the boundaries of traditional art and celebrating the essence of everyday life. It was a time when artists sought to break free from the confines of elitism, embracing the mundane, and elevating it to the status of high art.

As you delve into these pages, you will witness how simple pictures are reimagined and immortalized through the eyes of Pop Art. This collection embraces the spirit of the movement—accessible, dynamic, and brimming with undeniable charisma.

The Pop Art Flowers Collection invites you to join a revolution—an artistic rebellion that challenged conventions, shattered norms, and left an indelible mark on the canvas of history. Each poster captured the zeitgeist of its time, leaving us with timeless snapshots of an era that dared to dream and redefine.

Welcome to The Pop Art Flowers Collection—a testament to the eternal allure of an artistic movement that forever echoes the beating pulse of our modern world. Let these posters ignite your imagination and inspire you to find beauty in the simplest, yet most extraordinary aspects of life.

Enjoy the ride!

# HOW TO CUT THE ART PRINTS

Cutting an art prints with precision is essential to achieve a clean result. Whether you're creating a collage, framing the prints, or using it for a creative project, following these step-by-step instructions will ensure you make accurate cuts using scissors and the broken lines on the art prints.

## Materials Needed

- Scissors with sharp blades

## Step-by-Step Instructions

*Prepare Your Workspace* - Choose a well-lit and clean workspace to avoid any accidental damage to the art print. Lay the book flat on a smooth surface, ensuring there are no creases or wrinkles.

*Examine the Art Print* -Look for any pre-existing  broken lines . All the art prints in this book  have printed guidelines that can serve as cutting guides.

*Align the Scissors* - Hold the scissors parallel to the cutting lines . Make sure the blades are aligned with the lines to ensure a straight cut. Follow the pre-existing lines closely to maintain the intended design.

*Start Cutting* -With a steady hand, begin cutting along the marked lines. Work slowly and smoothly, allowing the scissors to glide along the paper.

*Check Your Progress* -Periodically check your cuts to ensure they are following the intended lines. If you notice any deviations, adjust your cutting technique and realign the scissors to correct the course.

*Dispose of Scrap* -Dispose of any excess paper or scraps responsibly. If you plan to use the cut-out parts for other projects, keep them organized and store them safely.

**Congratulations!** You have successfully cut your art print using scissors and the broken lines as your guide. With careful attention to detail and a steady hand, you've achieved clean cuts that will enhance your prints's appearance and make it ready for your desired purpose.

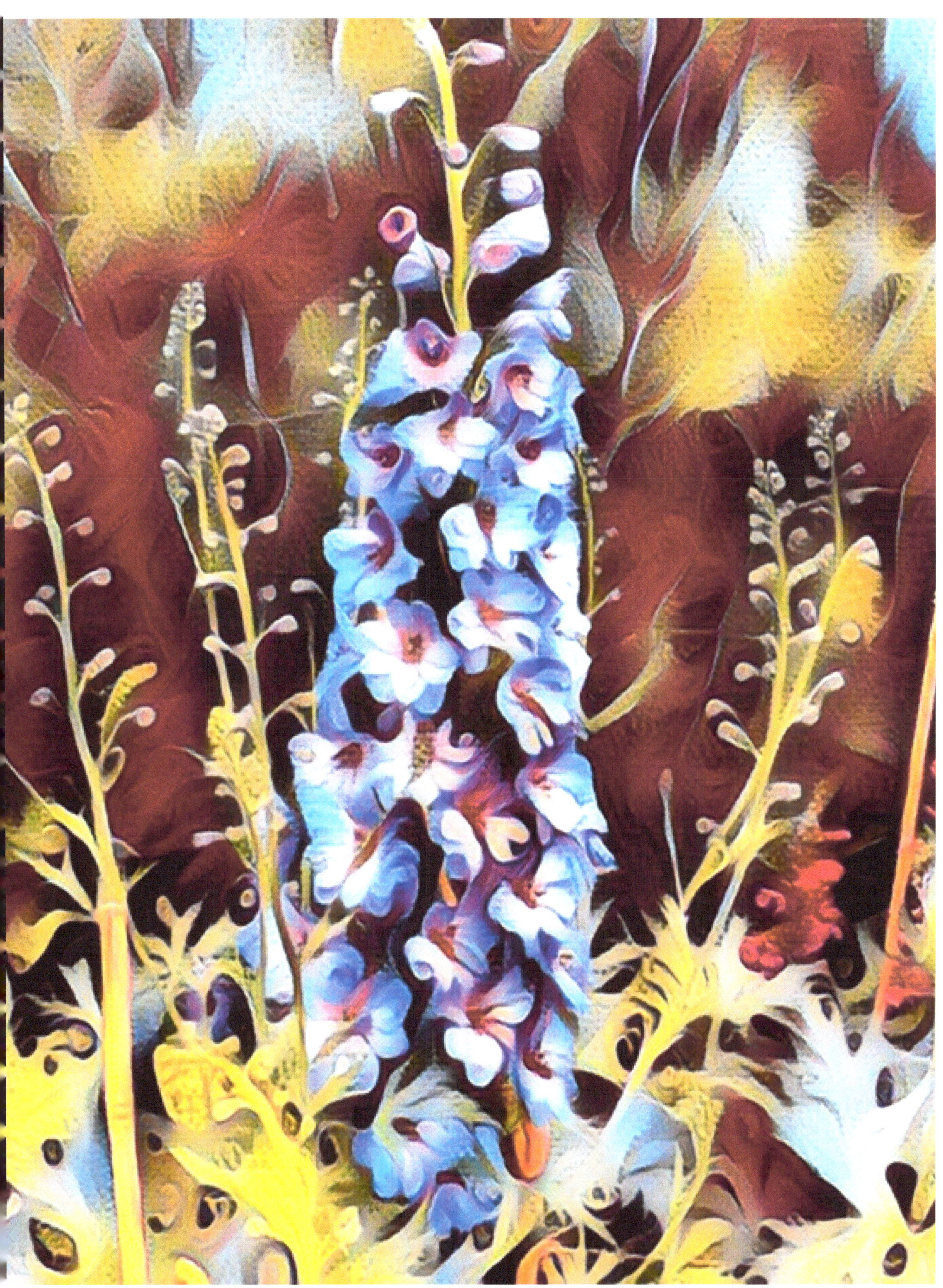

POP ART FLOWERS COLLECTION
**BY SABRINA MARTORELLI**

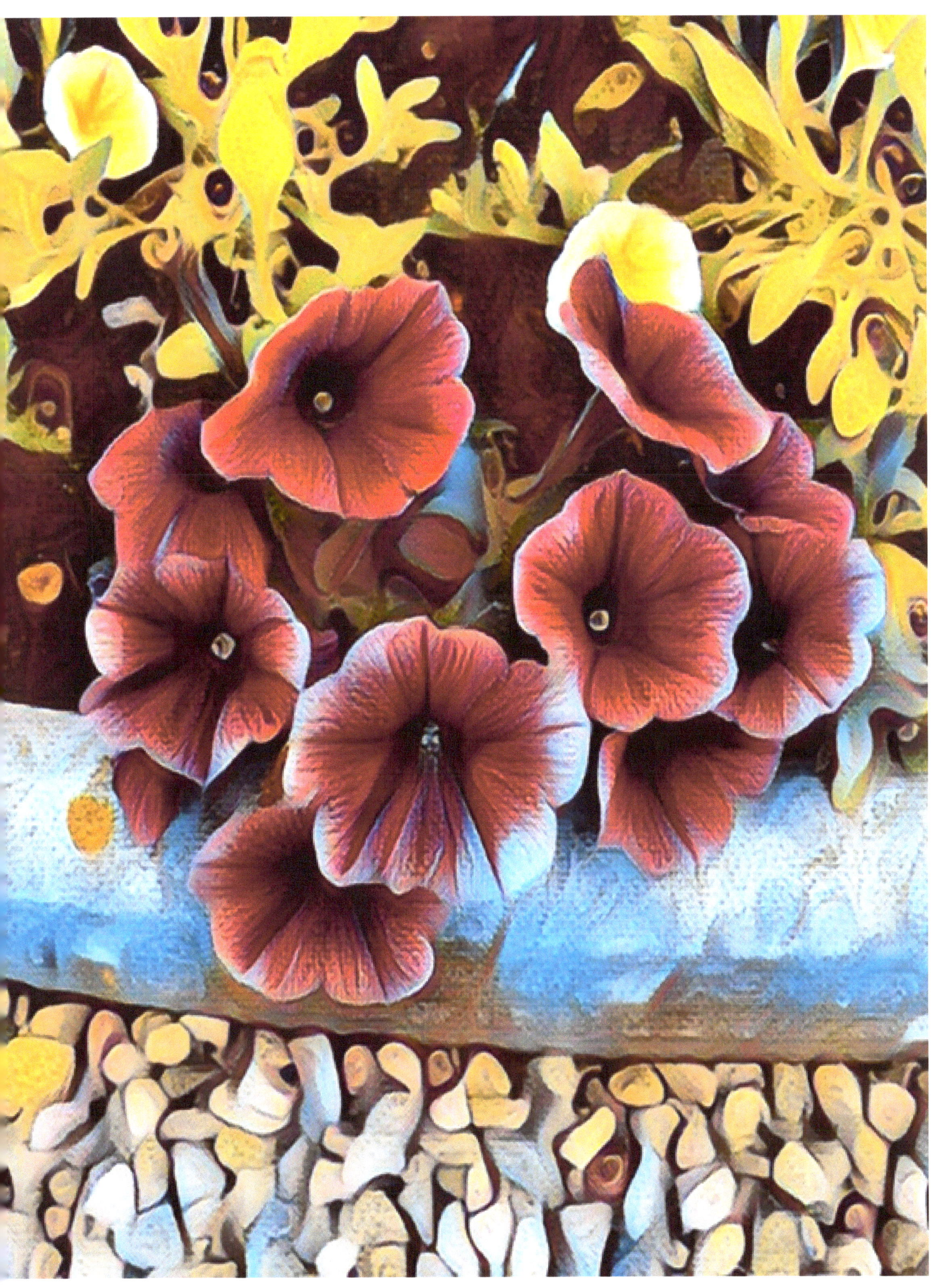

POP ART FLOWERS COLLECTION
BY SABRINA MARTORELLI

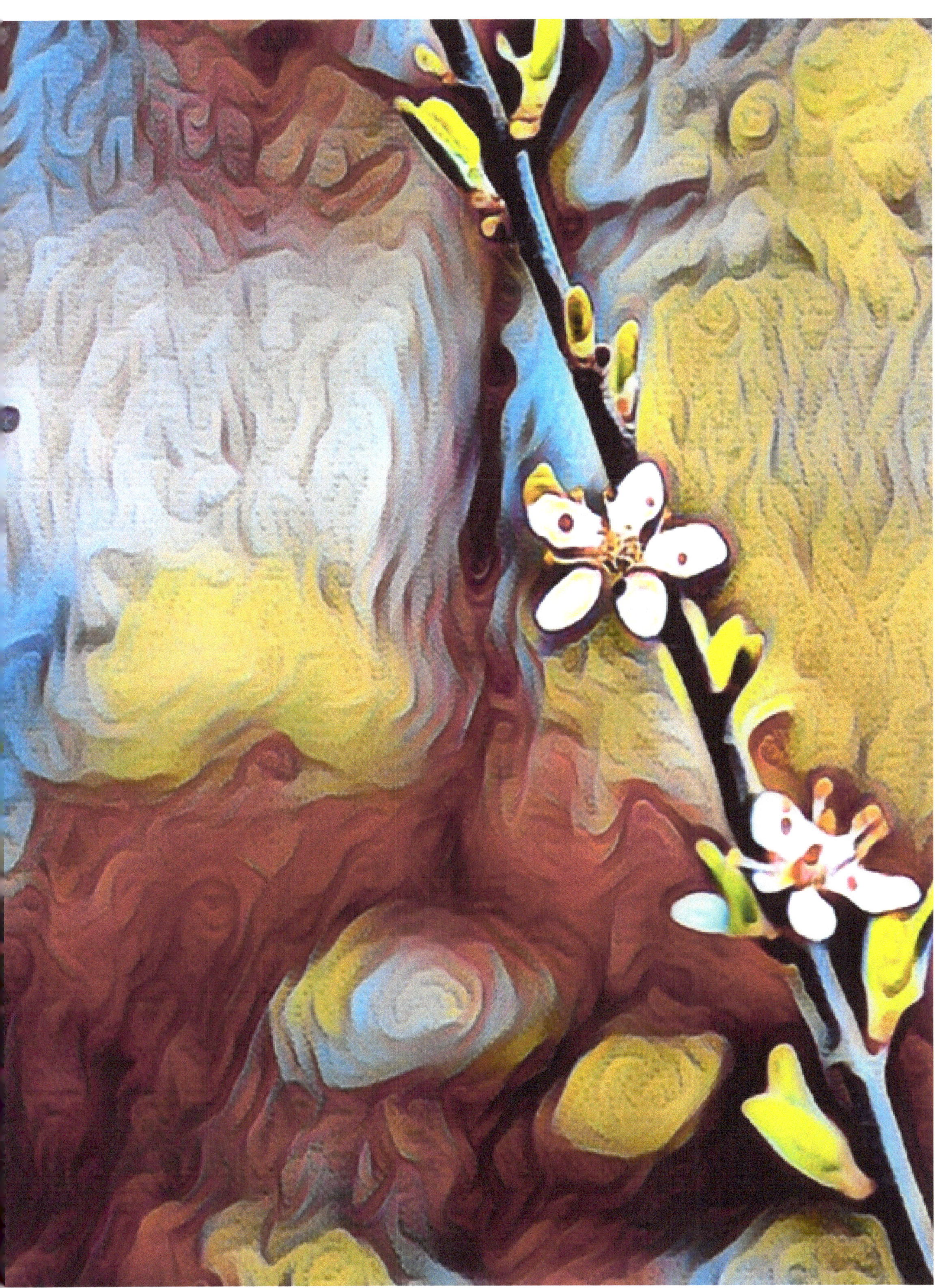

POP ART FLOWERS COLLECTION
BY SABRINA MARTORELLI

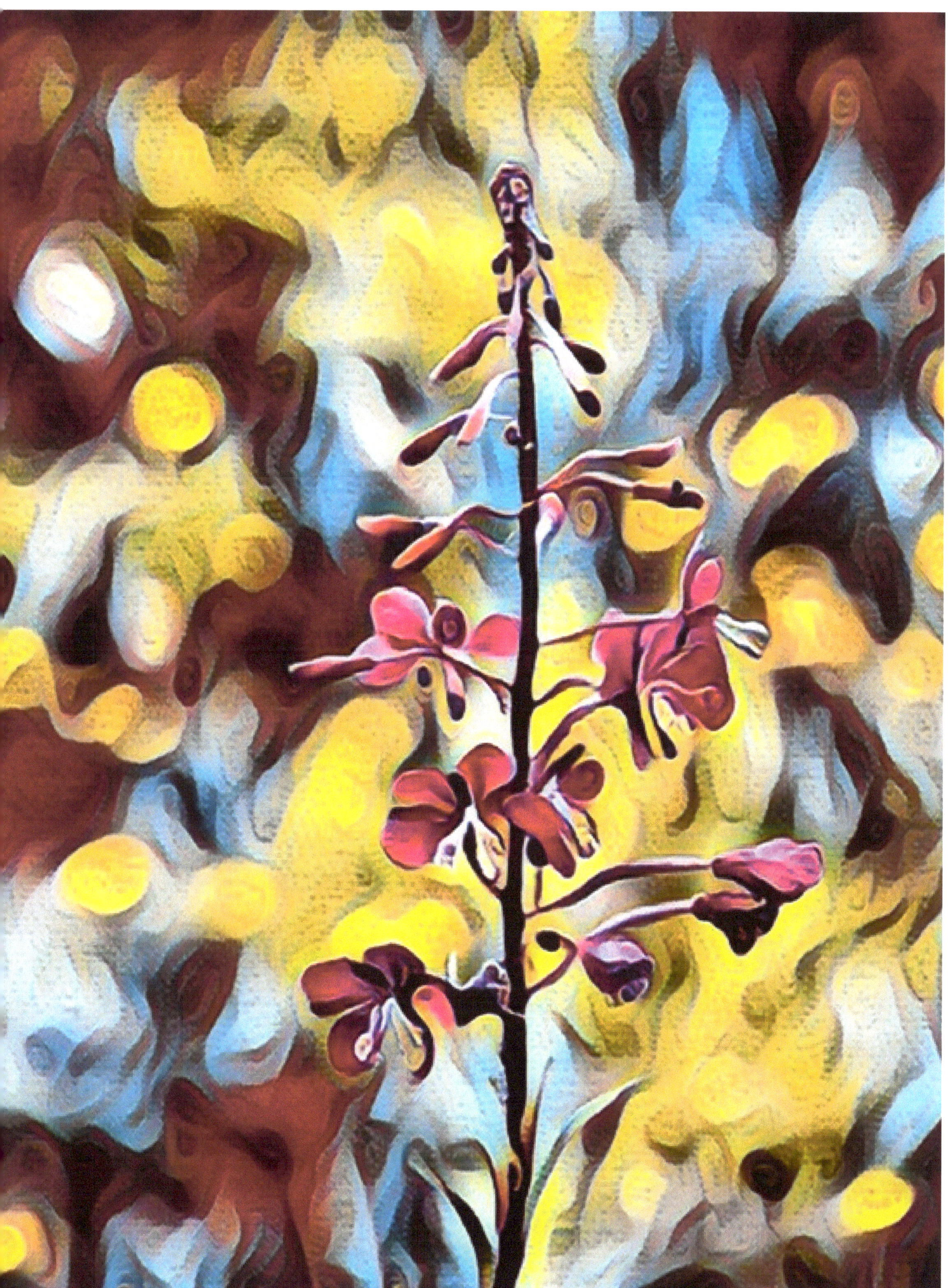

POP ART FLOWERS COLLECTION
BY SABRINA MARTORELLI

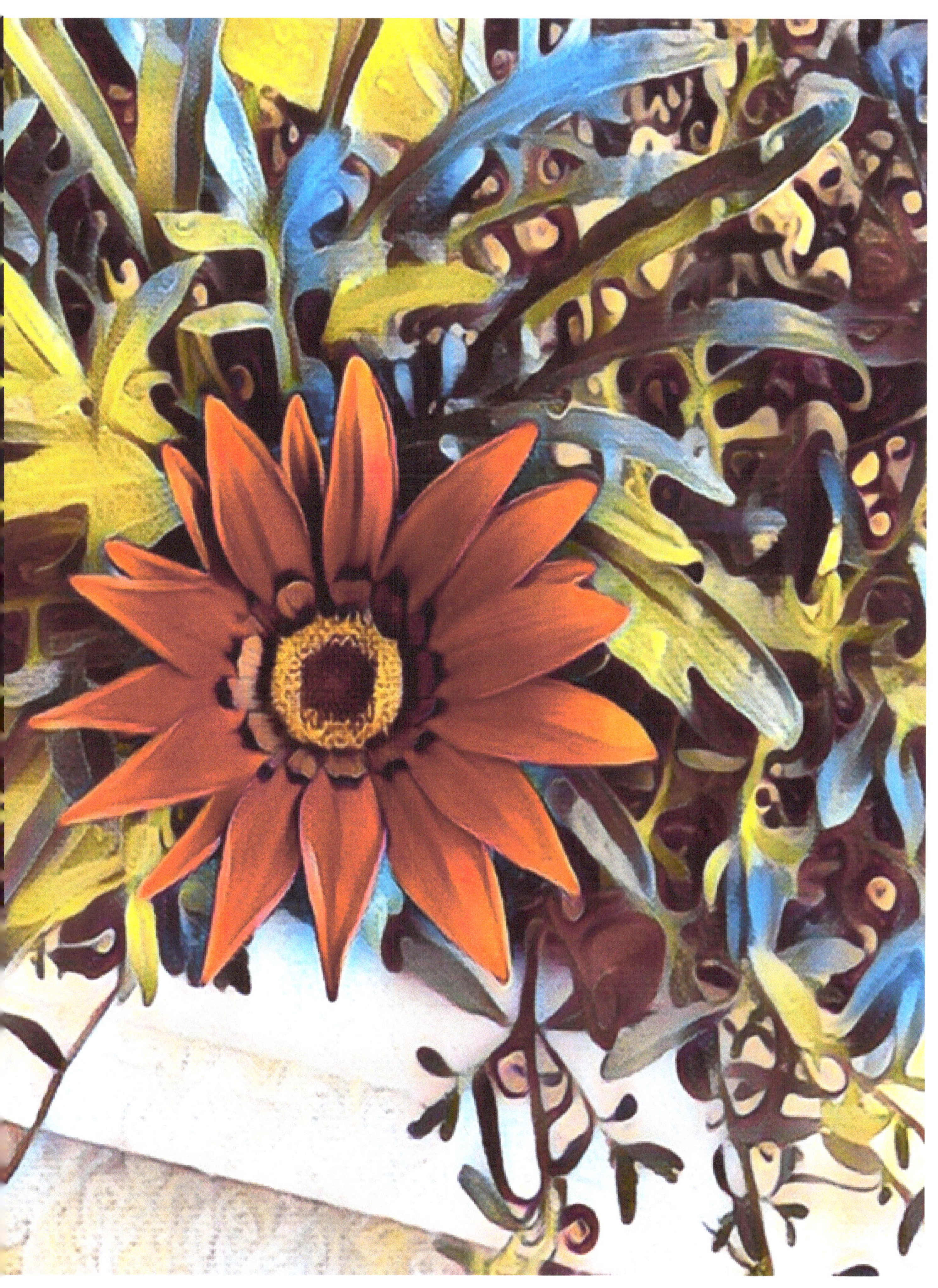

POP ART FLOWERS COLLECTION
BY SABRINA MARTORELLI

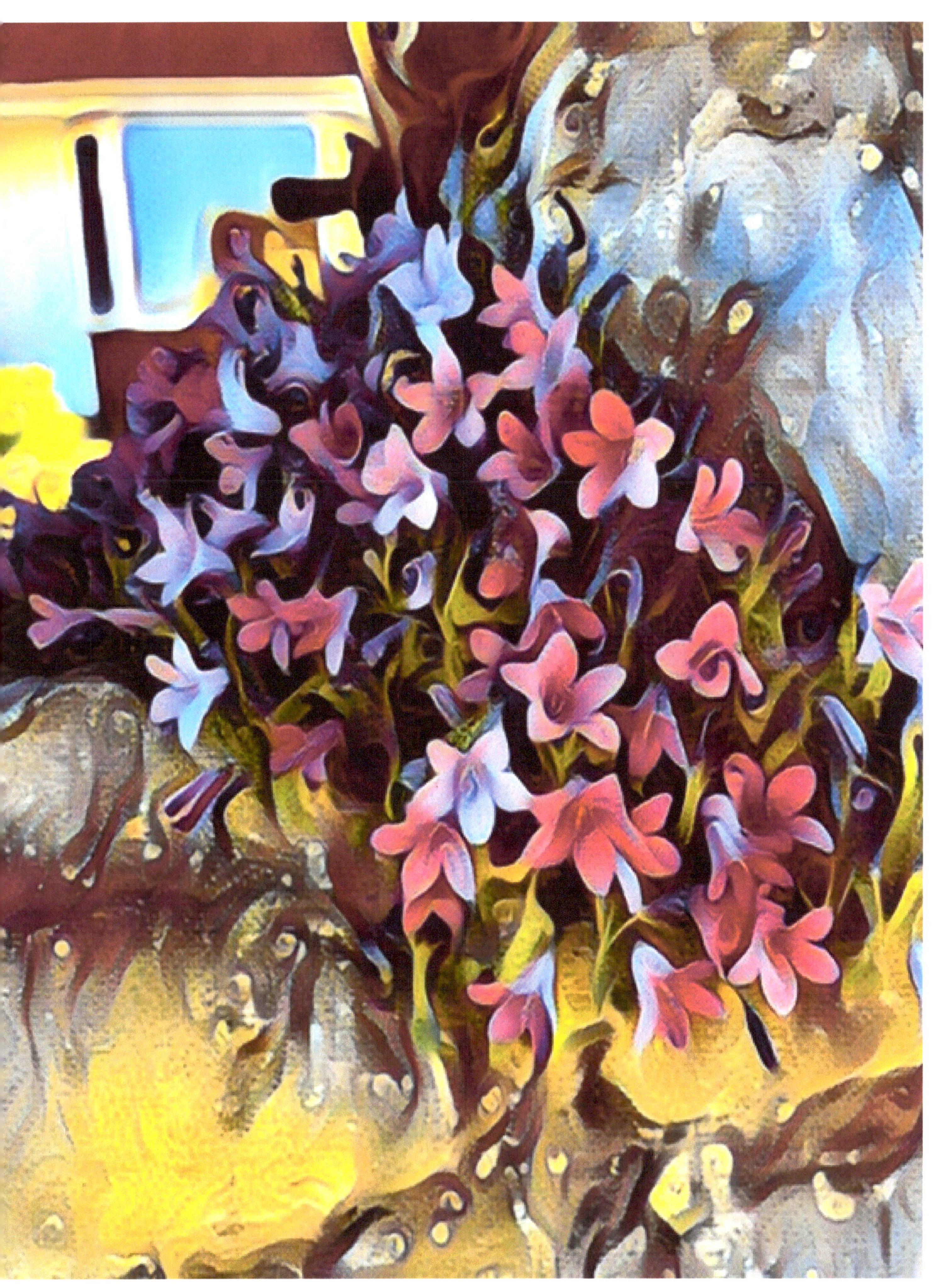

POP ART FLOWERS COLLECTION

**BY SABRINA MARTORELLI**

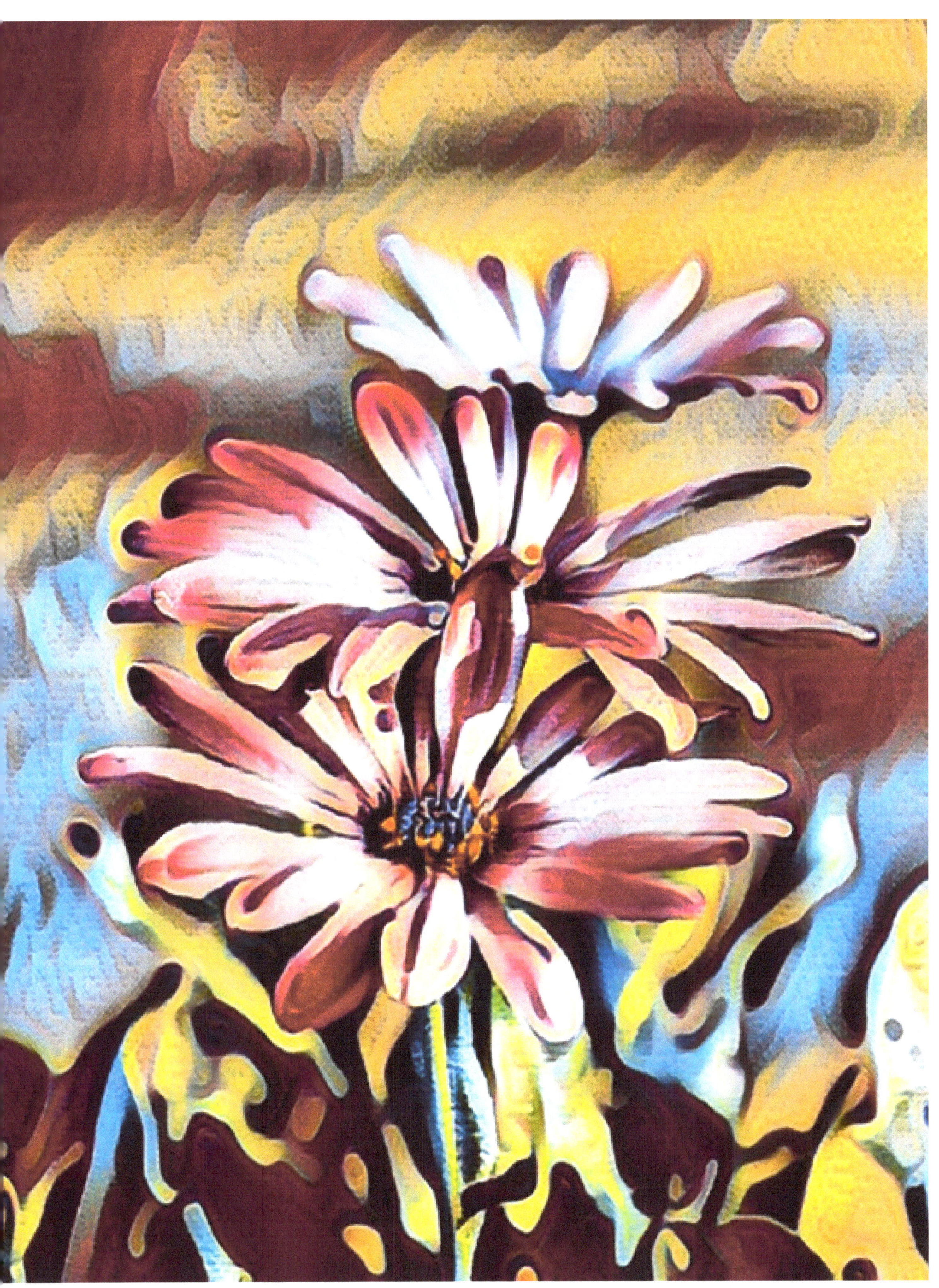

POP ART FLOWERS COLLECTION
BY SABRINA MARTORELLI

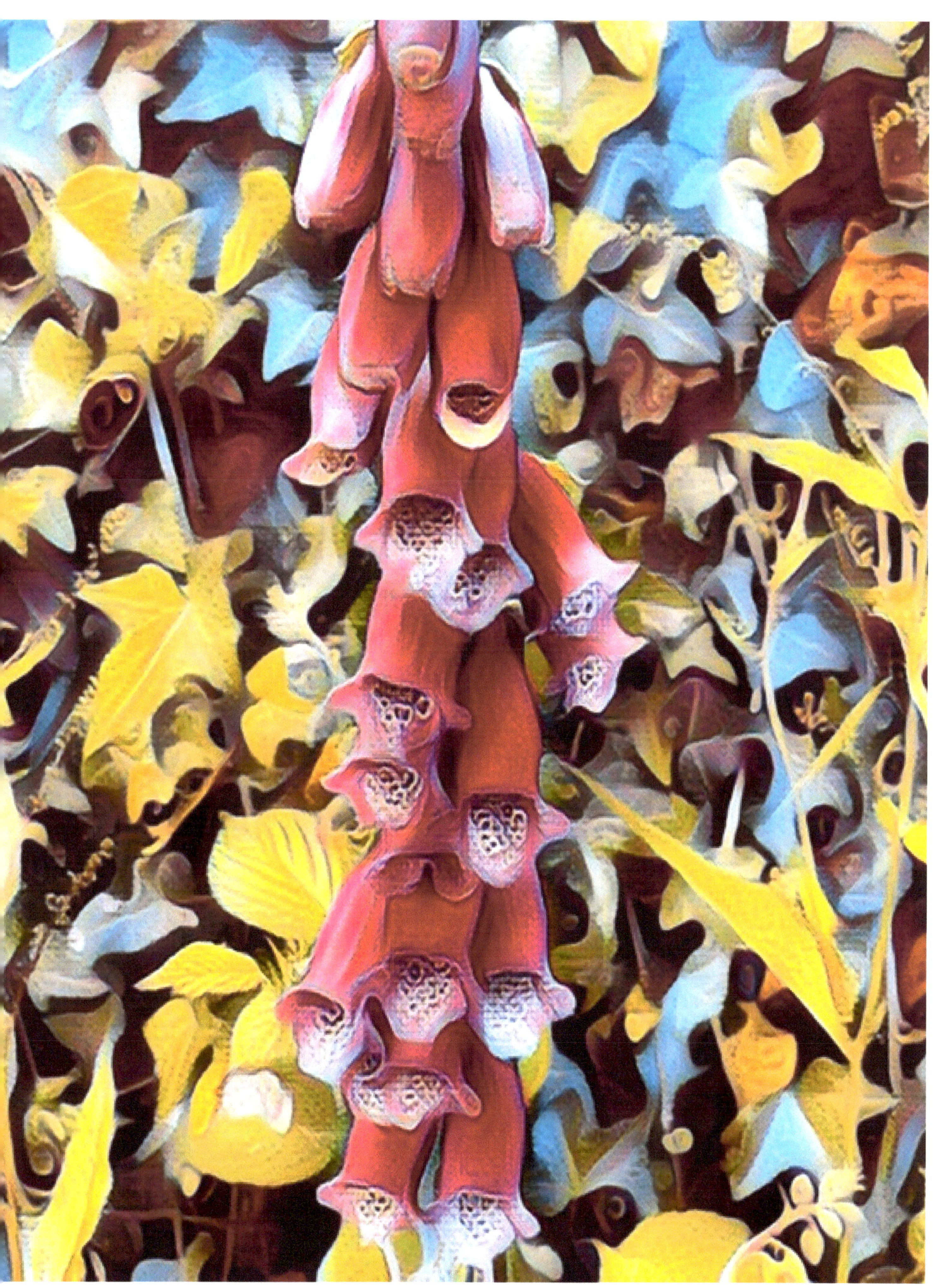

POP ART FLOWERS COLLECTION

BY SABRINA MARTORELLI

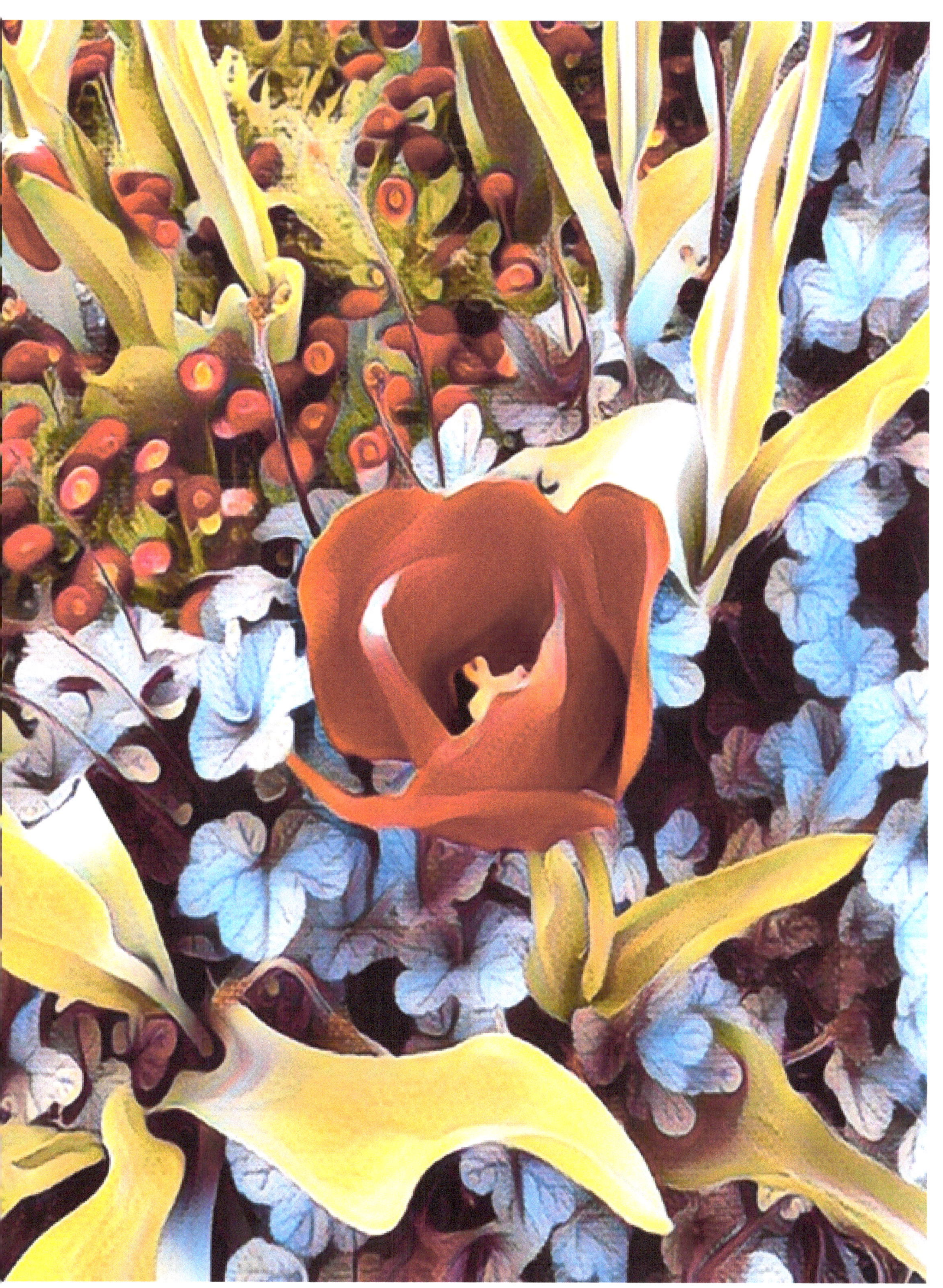

POP ART FLOWERS COLLECTION
**BY SABRINA MARTORELLI**

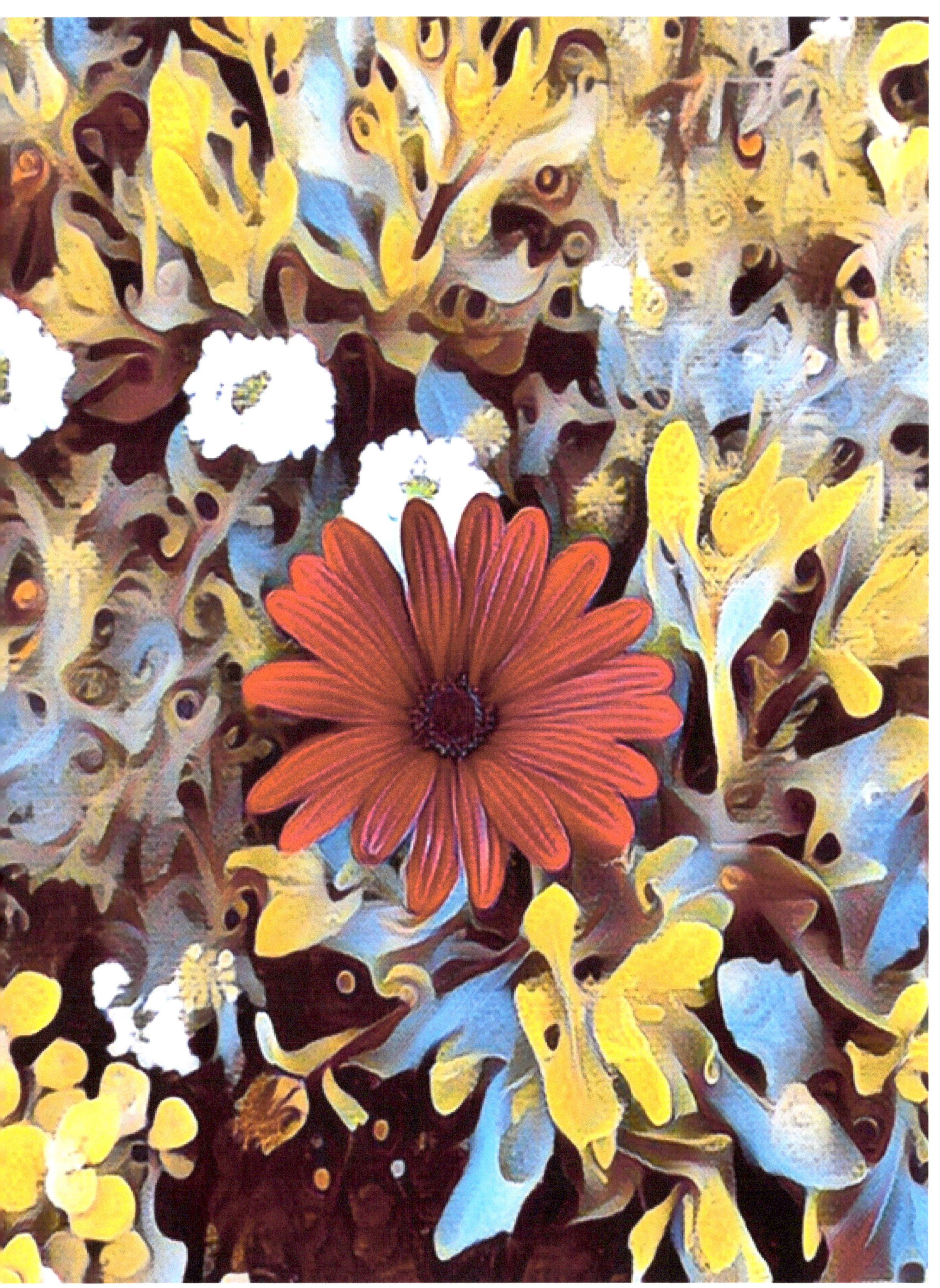

POP ART FLOWERS COLLECTION
**BY SABRINA MARTORELLI**

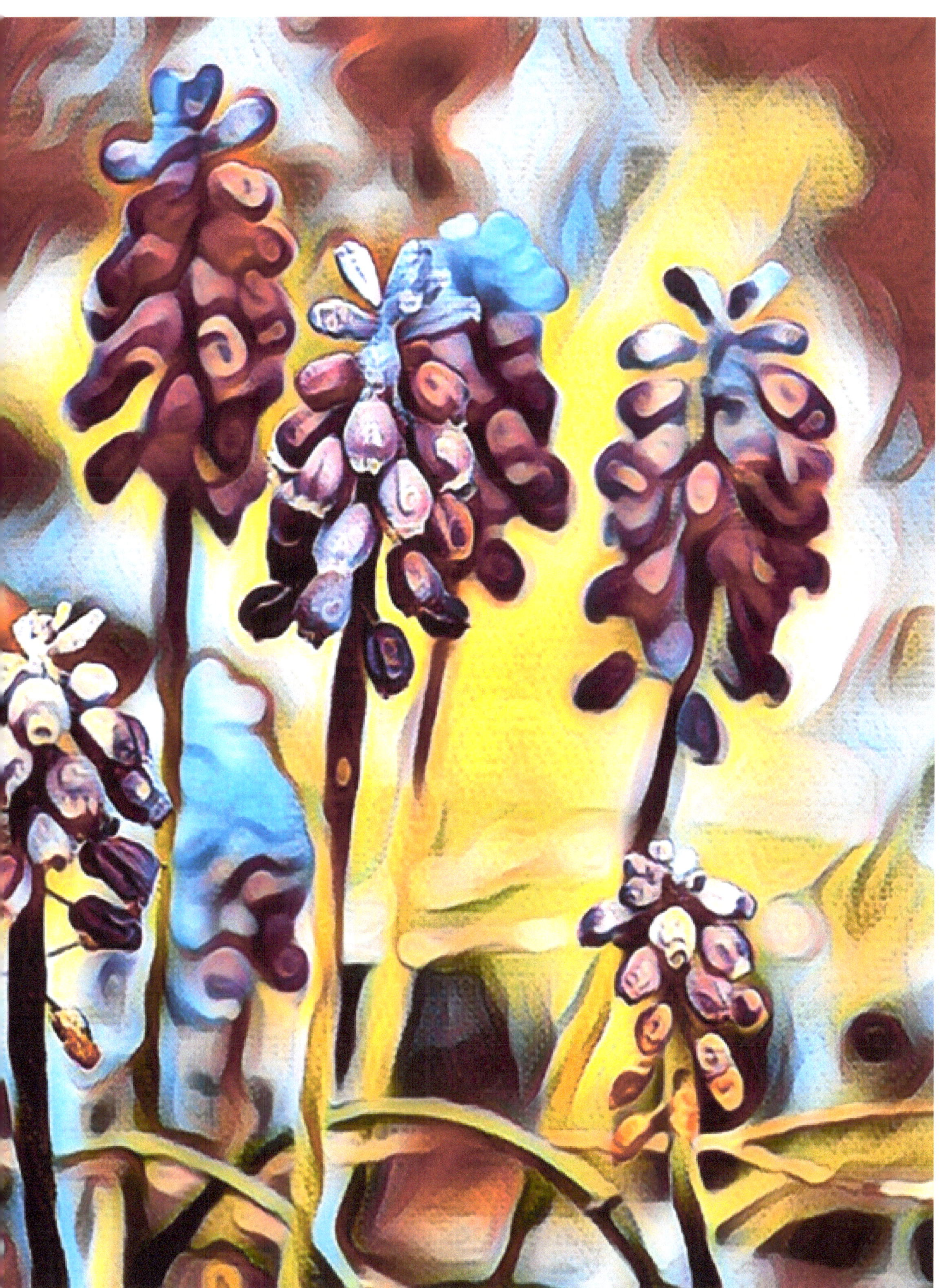

POP ART FLOWERS COLLECTION
**BY SABRINA MARTORELLI**

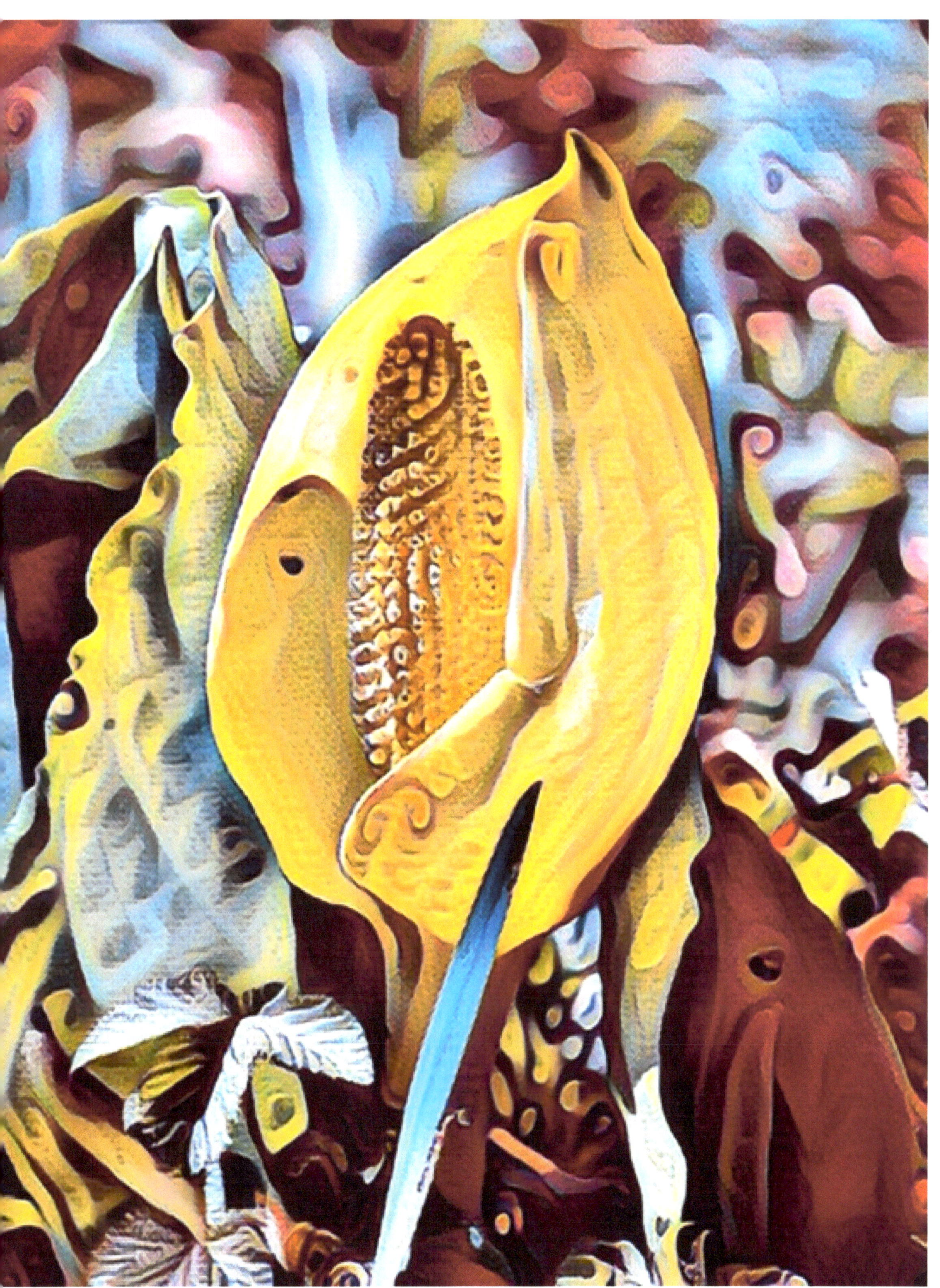

POP ART FLOWERS COLLECTION

**BY SABRINA MARTORELLI**

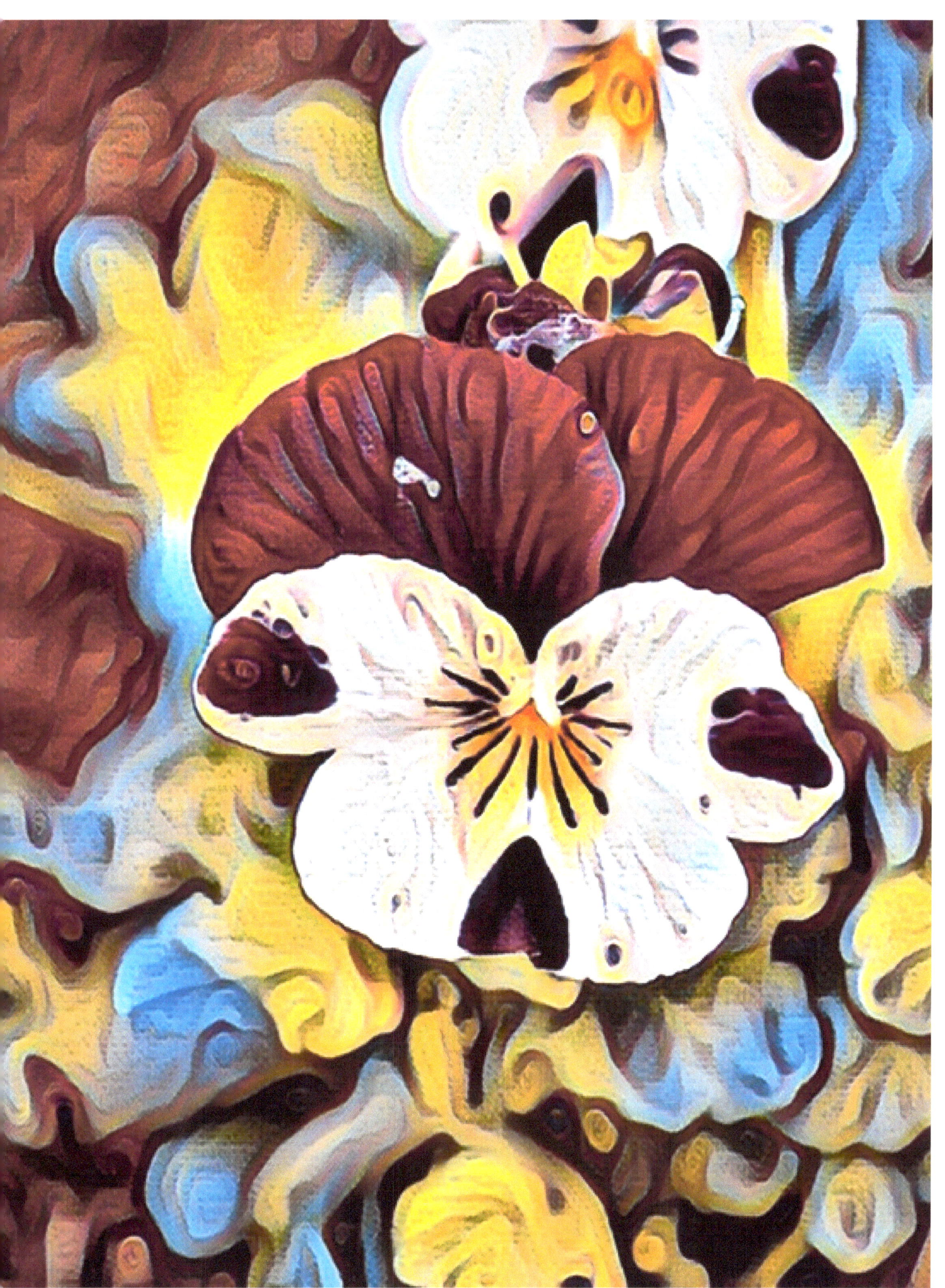

POP ART FLOWERS COLLECTION
**BY SABRINA MARTORELLI**

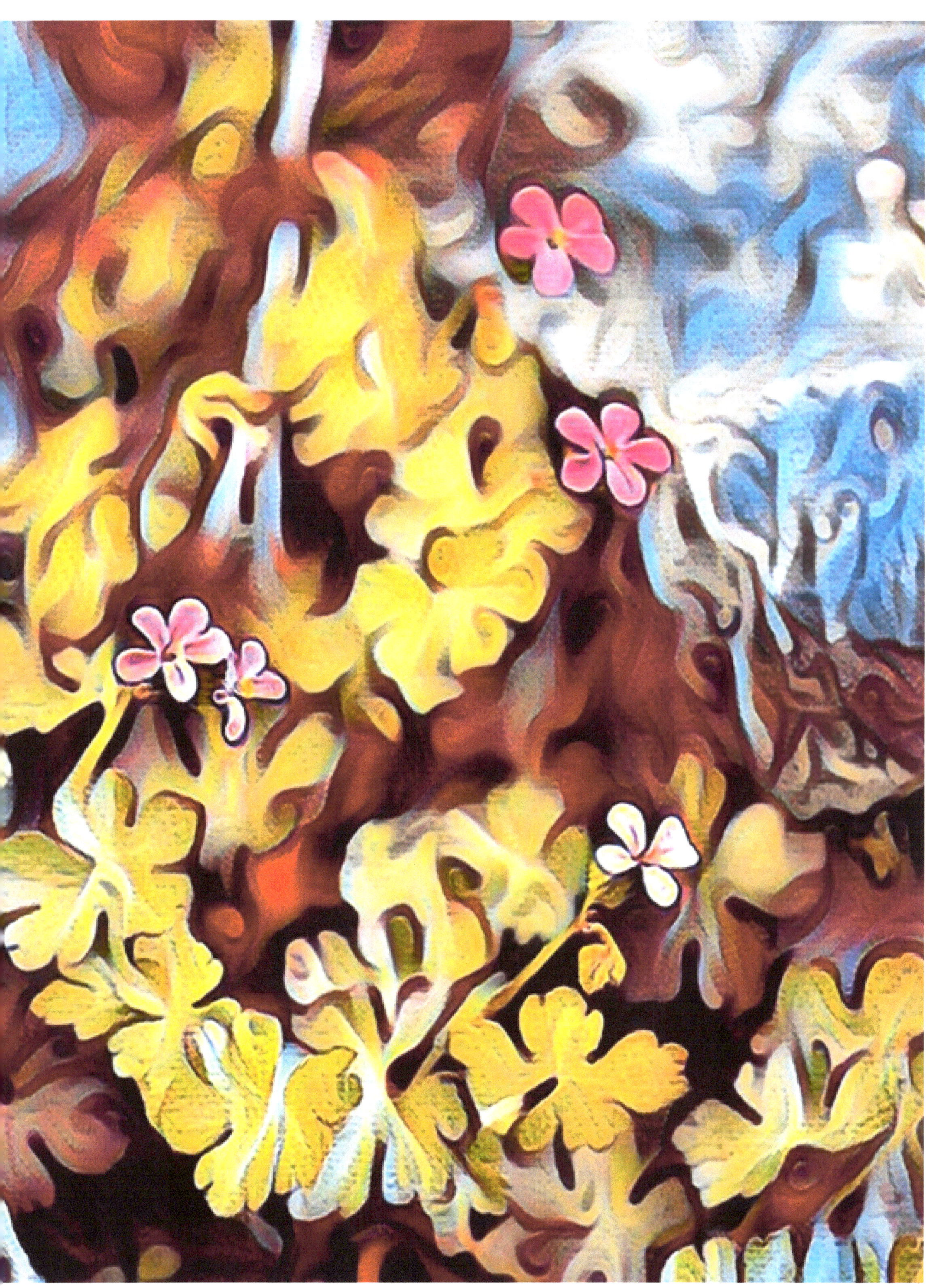

POP ART FLOWERS COLLECTION
BY SABRINA MARTORELLI

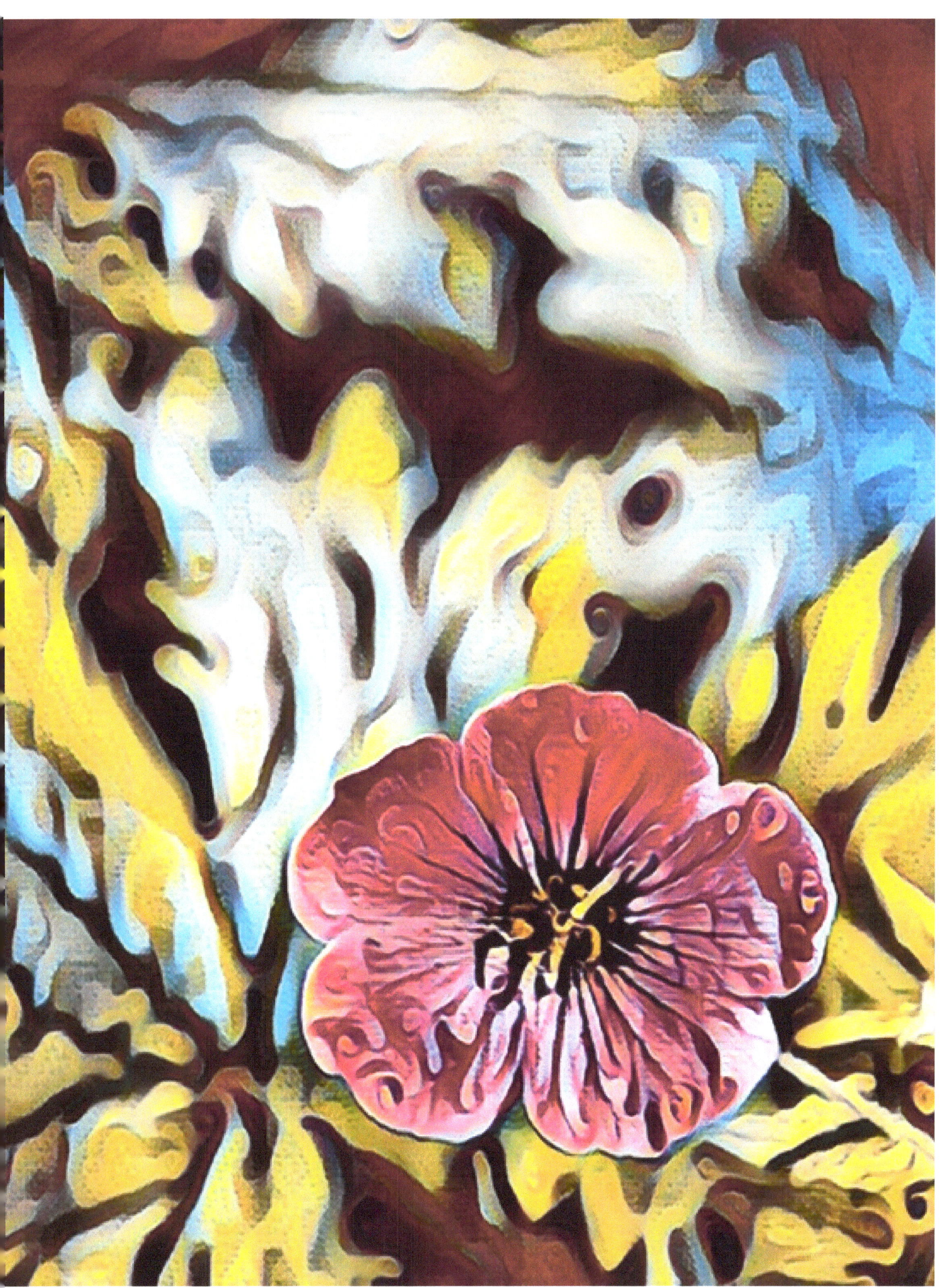

POP ART FLOWERS COLLECTION

**BY SABRINA MARTORELLI**

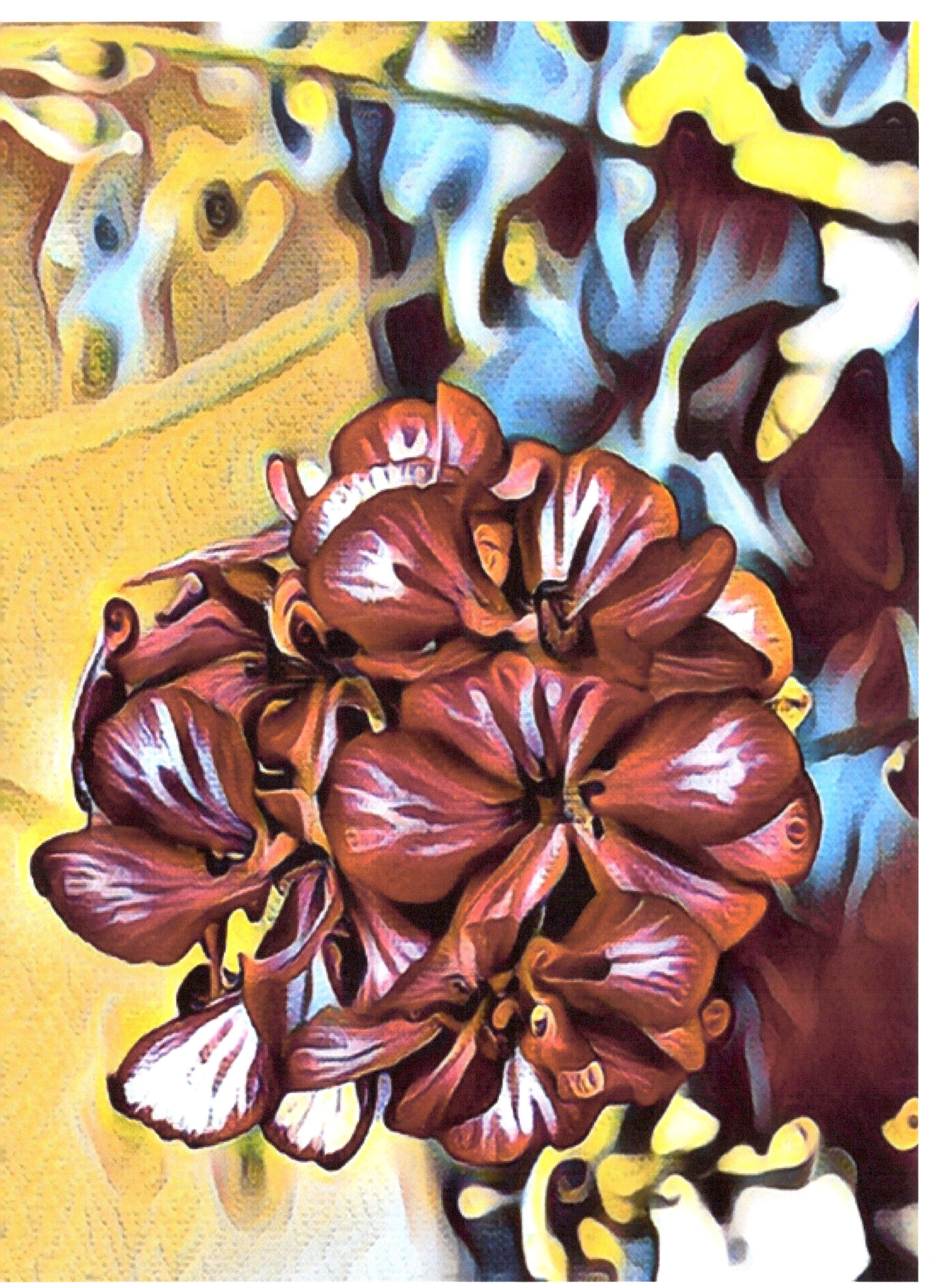

POP ART FLOWERS COLLECTION
BY SABRINA MARTORELLI

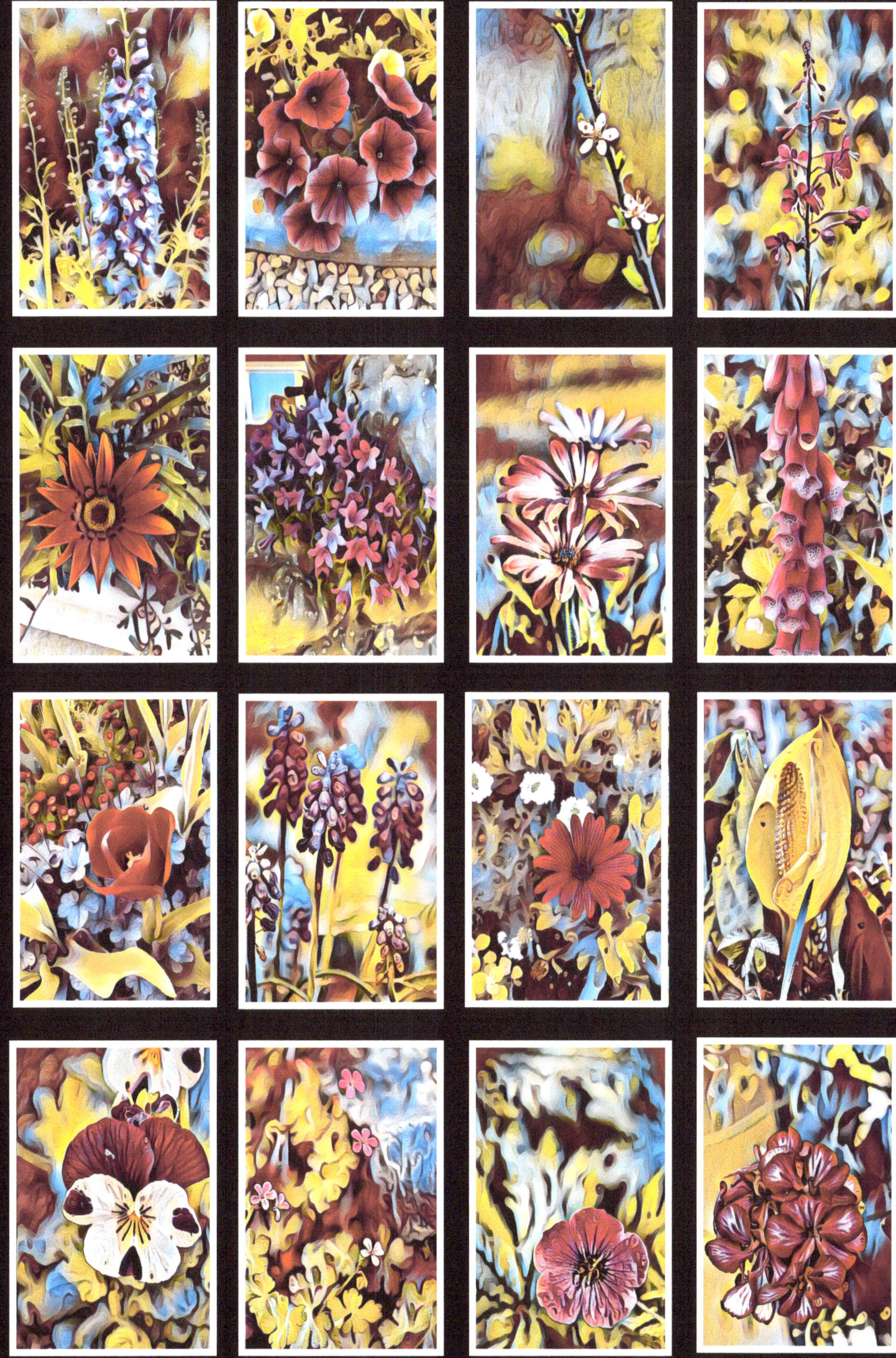

POP ART FLOWERS COLLECTION
BY SABRINA MARTORELLI

www.ingramcontent.com/pod-product-compliance
Lightning Source LLC
Chambersburg PA
CBHW040051240726

48664CB00004B/1146